Teensy Weensy Animals

By Joan Emerson

Scholastic Inc.

Photo Credits ©: Alamy Images: 10 (blickwinkel), 31 (C. Steimer/Arco Images), 1 (Idamini), 3 (Juniors Bildarchiv GmbH), cover top, 30 (Maximilian Weinzierl), 22 (R. Richter/Tierfotoagentur), 21 (Shinya Sasaki/Aflo), 13 (Zizza Gordon); Biosphoto/Cyril Ruoso: 8; CG Textures/Jason Hollefreund: 25 leaves; Christopher Austin, Ph.D.: 27; Dreamstime: 23 (Clinweaver), 6 (Fischer0182), 28 (Ian Poole), 11 (Mgkuijpers); Fotolia/Hiro: 20; Getty Images/Mike Simons: 7; iStockphoto/blackred: cover bottom; Lucy Cooke: 5; Minden Pictures: 17 (Daniel Heuclin), 16 (Dietmar Nill), 12 (Michael & Patricia Fogden); National Geographic Creative/Joel Sartore: 24, 25; Newscom/Thais Llorca/EFE: 18, 19; Shutterstock, Inc./Leelakajonkij: 9; Thinkstock/jacus: 29; Visuals Unlimited/ Hal Beral: 15.

ISBN 978-0-545-75183-4

10 9 8 7 6 5 4   15 16 17 18 19 20/0

Printed in the U.S.A.   40
First printing, January 2015

Animals come in all shapes and sizes. Some are big, some are small, some are short, and some are tall! This book will introduce you to some of the smallest creatures from the air, land, and sea. If you look carefully, you'll find that teensy weensy animals are all around!

Dwarf Sloth

Would you believe that as a baby, the dwarf sloth is shorter than an adult human's finger? Even when it is full-grown, it will still be small enough to fit in the palm of your hand! Yet the dwarf sloth is special for more than just its small size. For one thing, its fur is slightly green! Also, this little guy can turn his head all the way around!

Sumatran Rhino

Usually, the rhinoceros is not considered a small animal. An adult African rhino weighs more than a pickup truck! But the Sumatran rhino is six times smaller than its giant rhino relatives. The littlest member of the rhino **species** lives in the rain forests of Southeast Asia, and has **existed** for over one million years. But today there are fewer than 300 left in the whole world.

Fairy Penguin

This tiny penguin is the smallest of all seventeen penguin species. It is just slightly larger than a carton of eggs! Usually, a penguin's feathers are black and white, but the fairy penguin has spots of blue, too. While many penguins live in the snow and ice of Antarctica, the fairy penguin makes its home in Australia and New Zealand.

Dwarf Gecko

The dwarf gecko found on the Caribbean island of Beath, in the Dominican Republic, is the smallest known lizard in the world. It is less than an inch long—that's the size of a penny! Like bigger geckos, the dwarf gecko has **transparent** eyelids. To keep them clean, they lick their eyelids with their tongues!

Silky Anteater

The silky anteater lives in the tropical **rain forests** of Mexico and South America. This tiny animal is the smallest of all anteater species. It is no longer than a pencil! The silky anteater travels through trees by using its tail to swing from branch to branch. And of course, like other anteaters, it eats mostly ants. It can **devour** up to 8,000 ants in just one night!

Wolfi Octopus

The wolfi octopus lives in the Indian and Pacific Oceans, and is the smallest of all 300 species of octopus. The world's largest octopus is as long as a school bus, but the wolfi is only the size of a paper clip! It may be the world's smallest octopus, but the wolfi still has eight arms just like all other octopuses.

Etruscan Shrew

The Etruscan shrew is no longer than a child's pinky finger. And it isn't only the smallest kind of shrew — it actually weighs less than any other land **mammal** on the planet! Yet this small animal can still eat a lot. The Etruscan shrew eats up to twice its body weight each day. That's a lot of worms!

World's Smallest Dog

As a baby, Milly the Chihuahua could fit in a teaspoon! Her owner wanted to make sure she was healthy and safe, so Milly drank milk from an eyedropper and slept inside a doll's crib. With her owner's help, Miracle Milly grew bigger and stronger. Yet she still only weighs one pound. In 2013, this earned her the title of World's Smallest Dog.

Munchkin Cat

The munchkin cat looks like any other cat, with one big difference: its very short legs! A munchkin cat's body stands only about six inches off the ground. Its legs may be short, but its personality is big! That's why so many people around the world like to keep this friendly and playful cat as a pet.

Pygmy Goat

Pygmy goats first came from West Africa. In the 1950s, they were brought to zoos in the United States. Now, a lot of people keep pygmy goats as pets! They are around 20 to 25 inches tall and about 50 pounds. That's about as small as a medium-size dog.

Royal Antelope

At home in the African rain forest, the royal antelope gets the crown for being the smallest species of antelope. Most antelopes are about the size of a small horse, but the royal antelope is only the size of a small lapdog. Could you imagine cuddling with one on your couch?

Paedophryne Amauensis Frog

There are plenty of small frogs in the world, but the *paedophryne amauensis* frog is the smallest. It is small enough to fit in the center of a dime! For a long time, no one knew this little frog existed. In 2012, scientists discovered it in the rain forest of Papua New Guinea. The *paedophryne amauensis* isn't just the smallest frog, it's also the smallest **vertebrate** on earth.

Roborovski Hamster

Dwarf hamsters are half the size of regular hamsters. And of all these little dwarf hamsters, the Roborovksi hamster is the smallest! It is shorter than a crayon, and can fit in the palm of your hand! Sometimes called the Robo hamster, it was first discovered in Russia, China, and Kazakhstan. Today, kids all over the world keep them as pets.

Glossary

devour: to eat something quickly and hungrily

existed: to have been real or alive

mammal: a warm-blooded animal that has hair or fur and usually gives birth to live babies

rain forest: a dense tropical forest where a lot of rain falls much of the year

species: a group of animals or plants that are similar

transparent: clear like glass and lets light through so that objects on the other side can be seen clearly

tusks: a pair of long, curved, pointed teeth that stick out of the mouth of an animal

vertebrate: any animal that has a backbone

Pygmy Elephant

Mouse, hamster, bunny…elephant? Elephants aren't usually thought of as small animals, but the pygmy elephant is much smaller than the elephants you see at the zoo! Found in the jungles of Borneo, the pygmy elephant has large ears, straight **tusks**, and a long tail that sometimes drags on the ground when it walks.